STEM CAREER CHOICES

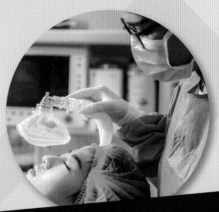

How to Choose Your Perfect
Healthcare Career

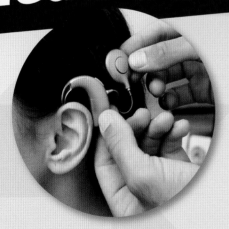

Cathleen Small

CHERITON
CHILDREN'S BOOKS

Published in 2023 by **Cheriton Children's Books**
PO Box 7258, Bridgnorth, Shropshire, WV16 9ET, UK

© 2023 Cheriton Children's Books

First Edition

Author: Cathleen Small
Designer: Paul Myerscough
Editors: Sarah Eason and Jennifer Sanderson
Proofreader: Ella Short

Picture credits: Cover: Shutterstock/Wavebreakmedia. Inside: pp. 1, 12, 18:
Shutterstock/Anek Soowannaphoom; pp. 1, 24, 29: Shutterstock/Peakstock;
p. 4: Shutterstock/Pressmaster; p. 5: Shutterstock/Monkey Business Images;
pp. 6, 13, 19: Shutterstock/Michaeljung; pp. 6, 34: Shutterstock/ZoFot; p. 6:
Shutterstock/Andrewshots; pp. 7, 41: Shutterstock/Ledomstock; pp. 7, 57:
Shutterstock/AshTproductions; p. 8: Shutterstock/AlivePhoto; p. 9: Shutterstock/
ESB Professional; p. 10: Shutterstock/AshTproductions; pp. 11, 18: Shutterstock/
Goodluz; pp. 14, 19: Shutterstock/Monkey Business Images; p. 15: Shutterstock/ESB
Professional; p. 16: Shutterstock/LightField Studios; p. 17: Shutterstock/LightField
Studios; pp. 20, 28: Shutterstock/Soorachet Kheawhom; pp. 21, 28: Shutterstock/
Wavebreakmedia; p. 22: Shutterstock/Sportpoint; pp. 25, 29: Shutterstock/Andrey
Popov; p. 26: Shutterstock/Andrey Popov; p. 27: Shutterstock/Photographee.
eu; p. 30: Shutterstock/Lynea; pp. 31, 38: Shutterstock/MDGraphics; pp. 32, 38:
Shutterstock/Photographee.eu; pp. 33, 39: Shutterstock/Shurkin Son; pp. 35, 39:
Shutterstock/Puhhha; p. 36: Shutterstock/Goldsithney; pp. 40, 48: Shutterstock/
Pixelheadphoto Digitalskillet; pp. 42, 49: Shutterstock/Kurhan; p. 43: Shutterstock/
Tero Vesalainen; p. 44: Shutterstock/Pandpstock001; pp. 45, 48: Shutterstock/
RGtimeline; pp. 47, 49: Shutterstock/Branislav Nenin; p. 50: Shutterstock/
Ledomstock; pp. 51, 58: Shutterstock/Marvent; pp. 52, 58: Shutterstock/
Ledomstock; pp. 53, 59: Shutterstock/Alpa Prod; p. 54: Shutterstock/Tyler Olson;
pp. 55, 59: Shutterstock/Tilialucida; p. 56: Shutterstock/AshTproductions; p. 60:
Shutterstock/VH-studio; p. 61: Shutterstock/Cookie Studio..

Printed in China

Please visit our website,
www.cheritonchildrensbooks.com
to see more of our high-quality books.

CONTENTS

CHAPTER ONE

WHO DO YOU THINK YOU ARE?

If you are interested in healthcare, then this is the book for you. Maybe you like helping people or maybe you find the study of the human body and its processes interesting. Perhaps it's a bit of both. Whatever the case, if you're interested in healthcare and what a career in the field might look like, you're in the right place.

Find Your Space

Having a general idea that you'd like to work in healthcare is great but there's one problem: it is a huge field. There are many, many career paths you can take within the overall healthcare field. Many require a college degree and even further qualifications but some require only specialized training, not a full four-year degree. However, this book is a good place to begin narrowing down your options. You can think about your personality type and then look at careers in the healthcare field that typically appeal to people with a personality like yours. So let's get started!

If you think you'd enjoy a career in healthcare but don't know what role might suit you, exploring your personality type is a great place to start working through your options.

The world is full of different types of personality. Different personalities suit different roles, and finding a good fit for your personality could help you make a great STEM career choice.

Follow the Flowchart to Fast-Track Your Future!

To find your personality type, you'll need to work through the flowchart on the following pages. The flowchart asks you simple questions to help you determine your personality type. This is based on five types of personality and the work situations that typically appeal to people with those types of personality. The five personality types in the flowchart are: social; practical; creative; organized; and analytical.

These personality types correspond to five different work environments. Social people, for example, often enjoy helper types of careers. Practical people often thrive in builder types of jobs. Creative people flourish in creator roles.

Organized people typically enjoy organizational roles. And analytical people usually gravitate to thinking jobs. Although flowcharts are not foolproof, the one in this book should help steer you in the right direction.

Exploring your personality type and career options is important because if you work in an area that is a good fit for you, you will be more likely to be satisfied and successful. And that, in turn, will lead to greater overall happiness with your life. So take a look at the flowchart on the next pages and work through it to determine your career personality type. Then, follow the next steps to find your perfect career in the healthcare industry.

5

This flowchart asks you questions about your preferences to help you figure out which of the five personality types best describes you. It helps you think about what you like and don't like, and what kind of work might be best for you, so you can make sound career choices.

Once you have figured out what your career type is, take a look at the career choices in this book. Each chapter features some interesting careers linked to the personality types shown in the flowchart on these pages. A variety of jobs are explored in each chapter, along with a day in the life of one of the roles featured. Each chapter concludes with a checklist that helps you work through how you feel about the featured jobs and if they may be right for you.

Helper

Are you interested in helping people and the environment?

No, this is not an area I want to work in

Yes, I want to make a positive contribution to people's lives and the environment

Do you like working in a practical, hands-on way?

No, I hate having to be practical

Yup, I am super practical

Builder

WHAT'S YOUR CAREER TYPE?

Creator

Organizer

Yes! Check that box!

No, art's not my thing!

That's me!

Do you love having things in order?

No, I don't care about that

Are you artistic or creative?

Do you enjoy studying and thinking through complex ideas?

No, I don't enjoy complicated study

Yes, I love theories and thinking through ideas

If you have made it all the way to this box, try taking the test again—you can work through it a few times before you finalize your answer.

Thinker

What Did You Learn?

Did you discover anything new about yourself from the flowchart? Did you find a career personality that just seems to fit you perfectly? If you did, that's great but if not, don't worry. It's very common to find that more than one personality type fits you. Most people are made up of elements from several personality types—for example, you might be both social and organized—and that just means there are more career options for you to choose from.

Weed Out the Nos

Regardless of whether you found a perfect match for your career personality, you probably found some types that definitely do not seem like they fit you. If you're not at all interested in the practical, hands-on, day-to-day tasks, then the builder-type jobs probably won't be for you. You can go through and weed out the nos to narrow down your search a little further. You're not closing a door on those nos, though—you'll go back to them later and explore again.

What to Do with the Yesses

Once you've weeded out the nos and identified your best fits, you can work through this book to learn more about the healthcare careers that may be best suited to your personality type. Each chapter covers specific healthcare careers that often are a good fit for the given personality.

Personality testing can be a great way to discover more about yourself. Your results may surprise you, and encourage you to think about strengths and skills that you may not have thought you had.

Career Insight:
Nothing Is Ever Set in Stone

Always remember that nothing is ever permanent. If you enter a career and find you do not enjoy it, it is not the end of the world. You can certainly switch to another career in the field or even switch to an entirely different field. The important thing is to keep checking in with yourself and make sure you are on a path that feels right for you.

If you find a personality type that matches you from the start, great! But don't panic if not. You may just be a more complicated mix of types—which might mean even more career options to choose from.

You can start with the chapters for the work personality types that seem like the best fit but don't miss the other chapters. When you've finished learning about the potentially good fits, go back and skim through the chapters for those nos you weeded out. You never know what career might resonate with you, even if at first that work personality type doesn't seem like a close match.

Explore Options

This book covers many options in the field of healthcare but not all of them. You can read the book to get started and then explore further. The Review and Check In sections at the end of each chapter feature further career options you could research. And once you reach the end of the book, the What Next? checklist will guide you through taking the next steps to kick-start your career.

CHAPTER TWO

HELPER ROLES IN HEALTHCARE

Healthcare is, by its very nature, a "helping" profession, so most people reading this book will probably enjoy helping others. However, certain healthcare professions more directly help people than others. For example, nurses work in hospitals, helping make patients feel better, while medical researchers are also helping people but they're doing so indirectly, from a lab. If you're the type of person who likes to help others by seeing them face to face, this chapter will have some careers that will interest you. Let's explore.

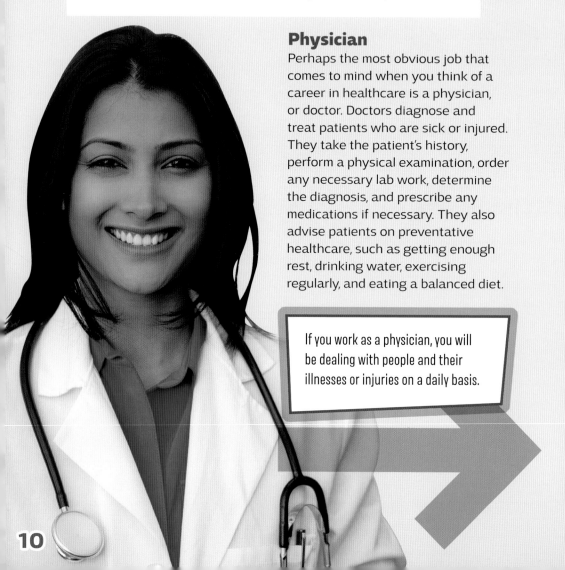

Physician

Perhaps the most obvious job that comes to mind when you think of a career in healthcare is a physician, or doctor. Doctors diagnose and treat patients who are sick or injured. They take the patient's history, perform a physical examination, order any necessary lab work, determine the diagnosis, and prescribe any medications if necessary. They also advise patients on preventative healthcare, such as getting enough rest, drinking water, exercising regularly, and eating a balanced diet.

If you work as a physician, you will be dealing with people and their illnesses or injuries on a daily basis.

It takes many years to qualify to practice medicine, and it is a highly skilled job that requires commitment.

Some physicians are general practitioners (GPs) who see all kinds of patients and treat a wide variety of injury and illness. However, there are also many specialties that doctors can choose to pursue. For example, surgeons perform operations on patients who require it because of injury or illness, while obstetricians and gynecologists focus on women's health and, in the case of obstetricians, deliver babies. Dermatologists treat skin conditions and gastroenterologists are specialists who deal with diseases and disorders of the digestive tract.

To become a doctor takes a lot of studying. You'll need to earn a bachelor's degree from a college or university that is accredited by medical school admissions boards. Following your degree, you must pass the Medical College Admission Test (MCAT), which is a test to assess a candidate's likelihood of succeeding at medical school. Once you've done that, you can apply to a medical school. Most medical schools use the American Medical College Application Service (AMCAS). This is a centralized application processing service from the Association of American Medical Colleges. Students select their target medical schools and submit a single application to AMCAS. AMCAS then sends the application to each institution. Medical school takes four years to complete.

To practice medicine, you'll need to pass the first and second parts of the United States Medical Licensing Examination (USMLE). After that, you'll then begin a residency, which will last anywhere from three to seven years, depending on the area of medicine you focus on. The final step in the residency process is to complete part three of the USMLE. Once you've done this, you can earn board certifications for your specialized field. Board-certified doctors must then apply for a state licence before they enter the field.

Anesthesiologists have a hugely responsible role to play in the surgical theater.

Career Insight:
Why So Much Money?

Anesthesiologists are highly trained specialists who, for each patient, must calculate exactly how much anesthetic to give and when, so that the patient falls asleep for a surgical procedure, stays asleep the whole time, and feels no pain until surgery is over and they begin to recover. Anesthesiologists are one of the highest paid of all physicians. This is because anesthesia is complicated as far as medication goes: Too much anesthetic, and the patient could die but not enough anesthetic, and they could wake up during surgery or feel the pain of the scalpel. Anesthesiologists also have very expensive malpractice insurance—because there is significant risk involved in this career, the malpractice insurance rates are fairly high.

Nurse

If you like helping people but you aren't inclined to spend around 12 years beyond high school earning a higher education, you might want to consider nursing as a profession.

Nurses are very hands-on with patients—often more so than doctors. Doctors typically see their patients for a few minutes at a time—maybe 15 to 30 minutes for an office visit, or 20 minutes a day during morning and evening rounds if their patient is in the hospital. Nurses, on the other hand, see patients all day long in the hospital. They are in and out of patients' rooms, taking their vital signs and checking in to be sure their patients are feeling well. In an office setting, too, nurses are the first medical professional that most patients see. Nurses often take the patient's history and current concerns before the doctor comes in for the patient's examination.

There are several different types of nurse. Registered nurses can have a bachelor's degree or a two-year associate's degree in nursing. They can also earn a diploma from an approved nursing program. Earning a bachelor's degree is the longest path to becoming a registered nurse but it will also open up the most job opportunities and probably

offer the best pay. Registered nurses who have an associate's degree or a certificate can expect to make a little bit less than nurses who have the full Bachelor of Science in Nursing (BSN) degree. Following any of these three paths, you must pass a state licensing exam before you can begin to work as a registered nurse.

Nursing Assistant

Another option is to be a nursing assistant. Nursing assistants must have a high school diploma and must complete a state-approved training program that is usually offered through a community college of vocational school. They provide basic patient care either in the hospital setting or in a rehabilitation or nursing home setting. Each state has a competency exam that nursing assistants must pass before they can enter the field.

Being a nurse can be a hugely rewarding job if you enjoy caring for other people and making sure that they feel reassured and comfortable.

Orderlies build great relationships with the patients that they care for. Like nurses or nursing assistants, they are often the people that patients in hospital have the most daily contact with.

Orderly

Similar to a nursing assistant, an orderly is a trained healthcare professional who works in the hospital or medical practice under the direct supervision of the nursing staff. Orderlies assist nurses by providing care and comfort to patients. Their job usually includes helping patients to dress and bathe, transporting patients from their beds to different departments for tests and procedures, and monitoring patients' conditions by checking their vital signs, such as blood pressure, heart rate, temperature, and oxygen levels. In the hospital, orderlies may also need to perform routine cleaning or disinfecting to help prevent the spread of disease or infection.

To be an orderly requires only a high school diploma but you'll need on-the-job training. Although their duties are limited, being an orderly can be a good way to gain experience in the nursing field while you see whether this kind of work is a good fit for you and before you invest time and money in schooling for a degree in the field. Like nursing assistants, orderlies have to pass a competency exam for their state before they can practice.

Career Insight:
Home Health Aide

Another option for those who want to be hands-on in the medical field but who do not wish to pursue college or vocational school at this time is working as a home health aide. Home health aides work with patients in their homes, providing assistance with daily living activities, such as bathing, eating, and exercising. Sometimes, the patients in a home health aide's care may have chronic, or very severe, illnesses but often, they have physical or intellectual disabilities. In the past, people with disabilities that prevented them from attending to all of their own daily living needs were placed in institutions or care facilities but that is not often the case now. It has been found that such people generally have a much better quality of life when they remain in their own homes with the support of an aide to help them with their daily tasks. As a result of this, the field is growing very quickly and in the coming years, home health aide jobs are expected to grow faster than the average growth across all jobs in the country.

For many home health aide jobs, you'll need a high school diploma or GED before you receive training. In some states, you'll also need to pass a certification exam. Being a home health aide is a very hands-on job in which you are providing direct care to patients and seeing the benefit you add to their lives, so it's very rewarding. This job is also a good stepping stone while you work toward another position in the healthcare field.

As the older population increases, there will be a greater need for home health aides who can help elderly people stay safe and well in their homes.

A DAY IN THE LIFE OF
A Surgeon

Although surgeons sometimes perform the same surgeries over and over, no two days in the role are ever the same. Every patient is different, and emergency surgeries pop up when they're least expected. These pages take a look at what a day might be like for a surgeon.

6:00 a.m. Surgery schedules always start early in the day. For one thing, patients need to have not eaten before surgery, and that's much easier when their surgery is in the morning. But there are also many surgeries to get through in a day, so it's best to start early.

6:45 a.m. You visit both of your early-morning surgical patients. You have to do a review of the procedure with the patients and their families before you get started.

7:15 a.m. You scrub in for your first surgery of the day: a gall bladder removal, or cholecystectomy. It's a quick, routine surgery that should last one to two hours at most.

9:00 a.m. Finished with your cholecystectomy, you head into surgery on your second patient. It's a colon resection, where you're removing part of the large intestine, which has been damaged. You're going to try to do the surgery laparoscopically, which means you make several small incisions in the patient's abdomen and perform the surgery through those incisions, rather than opening up the

Being familiar with the latest technology and retraining to use it is part of your job. Surgery technology is constantly changing and improving.

patient's entire abdomen. If you're successful, the surgery will be done in about 90 minutes.

1:00 p.m. You were not successful at doing the procedure laparoscopically. The patient was overweight and had significant scar tissue in their intestine—both complicating factors to the surgery. So, you ended up having to open the patient and perform the bowel resection the old-fashioned way, which takes much longer. You also ran into some complications with bleeding, but found solutions, and the patient is in recovery. The patient's recovery time will be a little longer but they should go on to live a normal life with a healthy remaining colon.

1:30 p.m. After grabbing a quick sandwich from the cafeteria, you start your rounds. This involves visiting and examining all of your patients currently in the hospital. You also get pulled in for a consult on a possible liver resection. You agree that the resection is possible and get it on the schedule for first thing the following morning.

2:15 p.m. A patient needing an emergency appendectomy comes into the hospital. Appendectomies have to be done quickly, so the appendix doesn't burst. If an appendix bursts, it can be fatal. You stop doing your rounds and scrub in on the appendectomy.

It's a quick surgery as long as there are no complications in the operating room (OR). It should be uneventful.

3:15 p.m. As predicted, the appendectomy went quickly, and you're now back to finishing your rounds. You have a lot to cover still, though.

4:00 p.m. A call from a colleague at another hospital comes in. She tells you she is working on a difficult surgery that she knows you've done successfully several times in the past. She wants you to come over and scrub in. You have operating privileges at that hospital too, so you go. You are happy to help out.

7:00 p.m. Finished with the difficult surgery, your day is finally over. But you're used to long days—it's just part of the job.

Assisting colleagues during surgery and overseeing junior surgeons is part of your role.

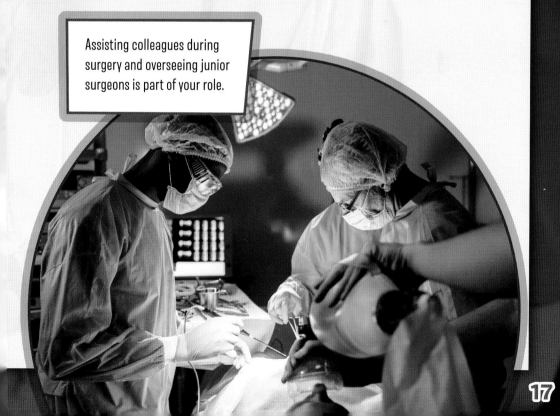

Helper

Now that you've learned about some of the helper roles in healthcare, explore more about how you feel about each job. Use the questions below to help you assess how strongly you feel each role might suit you.

Physician

- Why would you like to be a physician?
- What makes you well-suited to this career?
- What field would you like to specialize in and what skills can you bring to this field?
- Being a physician can be incredibly stressful. How would you deal with the stress that comes with the job?
- When you consider the lifestyle you would like in the future, does this job suit it? Why or why not?

Nurse

- Being a nurse is hands-on and often nurses do jobs that other people wouldn't like to do. What parts of the job would you find challenging and how could you deal with them?
- What personality traits and skills would help you be a good nurse? Are there things you could improve to make you better at this job?

"Always keep in mind what you want from your career."

"Make sure you choose a job that motivates you—one that makes you want to get up every day and go to work."

Orderly

- You need to be empathetic, organized, and able to follow instructions to be an orderly. Would that suit you? Why?
- What skills do you have that you think could fit the role?

Nursing Assistant

- Would you be able to work in a team of other assistants and nurses? What skills do you have to enable this?
- Would you prefer to work in hospital or a smaller facility? Why do you say so?
- Do you think you are well suited to working in a nursing home? What skills do you think you'll need to work there?
- What aspects of being a nursing assistant would be the most rewarding? And what would be the least rewarding?

"Always think, 'What am I good at?' then find a career that suits your skills."

Research More

If you like the idea of working as a helper in healthcare, but are not sure the jobs covered in this chapter suit you, here are some more helper roles you could explore.

Intensive Care Doctor
Paramedic
Midwife

CHAPTER THREE

BUILDER ROLES IN HEALTHCARE

Building might not seem to fit into the healthcare field because when you think of building, it's easy to think of jobs in construction, assembly, and similar. However, in reality, there are a number of careers in the healthcare field for people who like to be hands-on or make things.

Orthotist and Prosthetist

Orthotists and prosthetists do similar jobs. Orthotists work with people who still have all of their limbs and simply need some sort of supportive device to help them have full function of their body. They fit people with medical devices to help support them, such as leg braces or orthotics, which are special shoe or heel inserts, to alleviate foot, leg, or back problems. Prosthetists, on the other hand, work with people who have lost a limb to amputation or because of a birth defect. They fit people with artificial limbs to enable them to complete their daily living tasks.

Both orthotists and prosthetists work with their patients to determine the correct device to best support them. For example, there are multiple types of prosthetic legs, so a prosthetist must understand their patient's needs to determine which type of prosthetic would best suit them. Sometimes, orthotists and prosthetists build the devices themselves, or they might

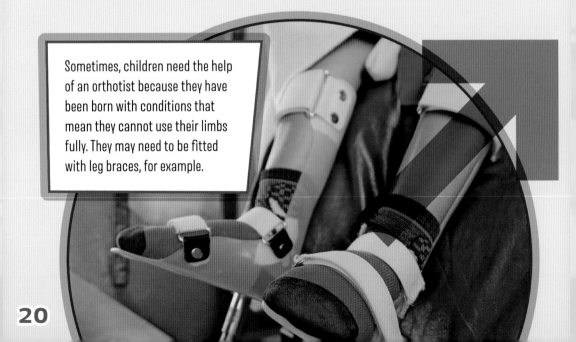

Sometimes, children need the help of an orthotist because they have been born with conditions that mean they cannot use their limbs fully. They may need to be fitted with leg braces, for example.

Fitting people with prosthetic limbs can greatly improve the quality of their daily lives.

work with a medical appliance technician (see page 22) who will do the actual fabrication of the device. Once the devices have been correctly fitted, orthotists and prosthetists also educate their patients on how to use and care for them. They also maintain and repair them.

Orthotists and prosthetists follow the same educational path. To qualify, you must first earn a bachelor's degree (usually in a science field or related) and then earn a master's degree in orthotics and prosthetics. Orthotists and prosthetists must also complete a residency in the field, which is usually one year.

The job outlook for orthotists and prosthetists is excellent. This is partly because the people born in the post-World War II years, known as Baby Boomers, have reached the age at which some are losing limbs to diseases common in the elderly, such as diabetes and cardiovascular, or heart-related, disease. Another reason for this positive outlook is because advances in medicine mean that more people are surviving catastrophic injuries that used to result in death. Although, more patients' lives are saved, they may require amputation to survive. And, as a result of the amputation, they'll need to have a prosthetic limb fitted.

Medical Appliance Technician

If orthotics and prosthetics interest you but you don't want to pursue college and a master's degree, you could consider becoming a medical appliance technician.

These technicians work in several healthcare fields, including orthotics and prosthetics, dentistry, and eyecare. They build, fit, and repair medical devices ranging from braces and prosthetic limbs to dentures and glasses.

Medical appliance technicians have created revolutionary prosthetic limbs for sportspeople.

Career Insight:
Weird But True Prosthetics

Usually, prosthetics are designed for function. For example, if someone is missing an arm, they need a prosthetic that operates as close to a real arm as possible. Whether it looks realistic is often less important than whether it functions realistically.

However, there are also people doing some very interesting, innovative work in prosthetics that goes beyond just trying to mimic the function of a traditional limb. For example, a student at the Royal College of Art in London, United Kingdom (UK), used a three-dimensional (3-D) printer to create a prosthetic thumb. The thumb functions as an extra thumb (rather than a replacement) and is controlled by pressure sensors that the wearer can activate with the soles of their feet. The Defense Advanced Research Projects Agency (DARPA) has also done work developing a prosthetic hand that can mimic the sense of touch by using electrodes on the parts of the brain that respond to touch, and the company YouBionic has created a double-handed prosthetic that can be worn on the arms to give the wearer up to four additional hands (two on each side).

Arguably, one of the most interesting stories is about a French tattoo artist named JC Sheitan Tenet. Tenet lost his right arm below the elbow and since he was right-handed, he had to learn to do daily tasks with not only one hand but also using his left, non-dominant hand. Instead of giving up on his dream to be a tattooist, he and his fellow artist friend JL Gonzal, created a prosthetic arm that had a tattoo gun mounted to it. With a little practice, Tenet could successfully create tattoos.

In general, to be a medical appliance technician, you will need only a high school diploma or GED. However, if you're interested in dental technology, you might need to complete a certificate program at a community college or vocational school. It just depends on the employer—some may require a certificate, and others may not. Training for these positions is usually done on the job. There are certifications available for some of these positions if you want to demonstrate mastery in the field but they are optional. However, as with any career, having a certification may open up some more doors for you as you search for jobs.

Product Builder

If you're interested in helping build medical devices, a product builder might be a position of interest to you. Product builders do exactly what their name sounds like: they build products. You can be a product builder in any sort of manufacturing field but if healthcare interests you, you can specifically look for positions in building medical devices such as pacemakers, cochlear implants, or hearing devices, and glucose monitors. Working as a product builder is just the job for someone who has excellent hand-eye coordination and can assemble products with tiny parts.

To be a product builder, you do not have to have a college degree. Typically, all that's required is a high school diploma or GED and good hand-eye coordination, good communication skills, and the ability to do fine, precise work for hours at a time. Some positions ask that you have previous experience in manufacturing, but other positions are entry-level, so no experience is required for those roles.

Biomedical Engineer

Biomedical engineers build or maintain medical devices such as X-ray machines and vision-testing

This girl is being fitted with a cochlear implant. Designing products such as these is a great job for people who enjoy making things but also want to help people in a healthcare capacity.

devices. Some biomedical engineers also work on pharmaceutical drugs, which is perhaps less of a traditional "builder" role but still involves creating something in the field. However, there are many opportunities in biomedical engineering for those who want to be really hands-on, working in hospitals, universities, manufacturing plants, government regulatory agencies, and research facilities. To work as a biomedical engineer, you typically need a bachelor's degree in bioengineering or biomedical engineering or in a related engineering field. Some positions require a graduate degree.

Product builders have a vision for how a healthcare product can improve the wellbeing of others.

Career Insight:
Industrial Designer

If you want to take product building a step further and actually design the medical devices product builders make, you may want to follow the career path of an industrial designer. They are the people who envision a product (often based on a client's request, though sometimes based on their own ideas), research the materials needed to build it and how it can be assembled, generate computer models of what the product will look like, and build actual prototypes of the device. Industrial designers work with engineers and manufacturers to determine whether the device is safe, reliable, functional, and practical.

And hopefully, in the end, their device will be mass produced for their target market and they can change the lives of many people needing that device.

To be an industrial designer, you'll need a bachelor's degree in industrial design, engineering, or a similar field. As medical technology continues to advance, there is room in the field for all people who can design these important products but the industrial designers who will probably have the most job opportunities in coming years, are the ones who have a strong background in computer modeling and computer-aided design and drafting (CADD).

A DAY IN THE LIFE OF
An Orthotist

As an orthotist, you will work with patients and orthotic devices all day: splints and braces, for example. Let's take a look at what a typical day might involve.

8:00 a.m. As soon as you arrive at work, you check your emails and voicemail and answer any messages that have come in over the weekend. Because you work in a large area hospital, every day is busy but no two days are the same.

8:30 a.m. Your first patient of the day is a young girl with scoliosis, a curvature of the spine, and you need to fit her for a back brace. Her spine curve is significant but not quite bad enough to require surgery so you fit her for the brace and recommend orthotics to go in her shoes. Orthotics have shown promise at preventing scoliosis from becoming worse and for reducing the hip and leg pain that can

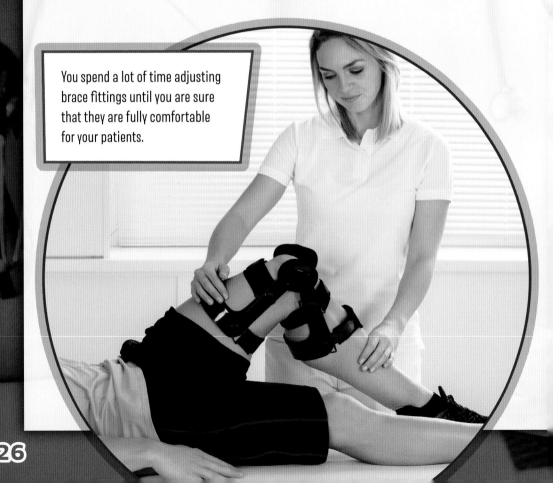

You spend a lot of time adjusting brace fittings until you are sure that they are fully comfortable for your patients.

It's so rewarding to know that your work changes your patients' lives.

come with scoliosis. The patient is having a difficult time with her diagnosis and is very upset. You spend a bit of time explaining to her how the brace will help her condition. By the end of the appointment she is calmer, but your next couple of patients are not happy that you're running late.

10:30 a.m. Your second appointment is to check an existing patient who has a leg brace. He is having some pain where the brace fits to the leg but a simple adjustment is all that is needed to relieve the pain. He leaves happy, and you're on to your next patient.

11:00 p.m. Your next three patients are all rechecks on braces. The patients are doing great, so the appointments run smoothly. You have time to quickly grab some lunch.

1:30 p.m. A man came into the emergency room with a nasty break in two places on his upper arm. His injury is going to require a custom splint and brace to heal correctly, so you head over to work on that.

3:00 p.m. The arm break was worse than you expected, so the splint and brace application took longer than you thought it would.

3:15 p.m. Your afternoon consists of several referrals from the podiatry department. Patients with foot problems are coming in to have casting done so you can create custom shoe orthotics for them. You spend the next two hours casting feet.

5:30 p.m. Your last patient has walked out the door, and you do a quick check of your email and voicemail before heading home.

Builder

Now that you've learned about some of the builder roles in healthcare, explore more about how you feel about each job. Use the questions below to help you assess how strongly you feel each role might suit you.

Orthotist and Prosthetist

- Trying to help a person to make their daily life easier can be very rewarding. What else about this work would you find satisfying?
- What do you think you would find most challenging about being an orthotist or a prosthetist? How would you deal with those challenges?

Medical Appliance Technician

- What aspects of the job do you think you would enjoy? Why? Are there aspects that you don't think you'll enjoy? How would you handle those?
- Are you able to follow a brief to ensure that the patient's needs are met? What skills do you need to be successful at this?
- What field interests you the most? Are you prepared to study further to specialize in this field?

"When choosing a career, always consider the career outlook—does your chosen area have potential in the future?"

"Think about the training involved in the career you are interested in. Are you happy to undertake it?"

Product Builder
- To do this job, you need to be excellent at working with your hands but creative too. Are these skills you are good at?
- What do you think you enjoy about working on medical devices? Are there specific medical fields that interest you?

Biomedical Engineer
- What attracts you to studying to be a biomedical engineer?
- What particular skills do you have that you think could fit the role?

"Think about what your work environment might be like. Would it suit you? Would you be happy there?"

Research More

If you like the idea of working as a builder in healthcare, but are not sure the jobs covered in this chapter suit you, here are some more builder roles you could explore.

**Dental Technician
Hospital Maintenance Engineer
Physiotherapy Technical Instructor**

CHAPTER FOUR

CREATOR ROLES IN HEALTHCARE

If you're a creative personality type and enjoy art, music, or other creative pursuits but you also think you'd like to do something in the healthcare field, there are definitely opportunities for you. Let's explore.

Medical Illustrator

Medical illustrators are talented artists who also have advanced education in the life sciences. They work with scientists, doctors, and other specialists to illustrate medical conditions and treatments. In the past, medical illustrators created hand drawings for textbooks, medical and scientific journals, exhibits, and presentations. Although that is still the case, most often today, a lot more of the illustration work is done via computer graphics. Medical illustrators are often animators because they create animated representations of processes for training and educational purposes.

Becoming a certified medical illustrator is extremely challenging because there are very few programs for it. To start with, you need a bachelor's degree in an art or science-related field, and then you'll need to pursue a two-year master's degree from one of the four programs in North America—three

Working as a medical illustrator allows you to combine your artistic talents with a role that helps improve people's health and wellbeing.

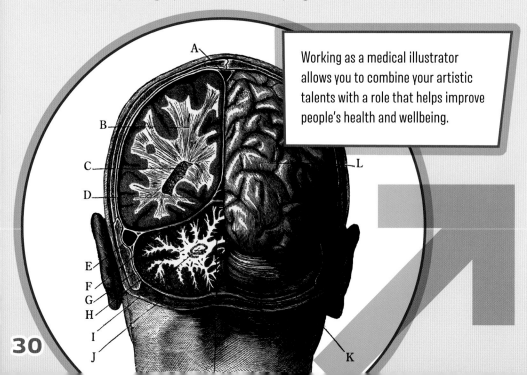

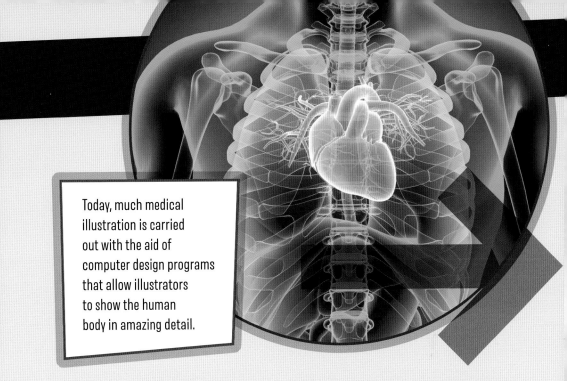

Today, much medical illustration is carried out with the aid of computer design programs that allow illustrators to show the human body in amazing detail.

are in the United States and one is in Canada. Because there are only four accredited programs, with each one taking around 20 students at most, earning a place is very competitive. Once you've completed your master's you need a certification offered by the Board of Certification of Medical Illustrators (BCMI), which must be renewed every five years.

Although you don't have to have the master's degree and certification to work in the field, without these qualifications, job opportunities will be few and far between. So if this is a field that interests you, you should aim to enter the master's program.

Music Therapist

If your creative passions lie more in music than in art, you could consider a career as a music therapist. Music therapists use musical responses to assess a patient's health, social

functioning, communication abilities, cognitive, or thought-related, skills, and emotional wellbeing. They also plan and coordinate music therapy sessions where participants listen to music, create and perform music, discuss music, write songs, improvise musically with a group, and more, as a method of therapy. While listening to music is fun and can be calming, it has been shown that music can also improve memory, stimulate communication, lessen anxiety, regulate emotions, alleviate pain, and improve motor skills.

There are bachelor's, master's, and doctoral degrees offered in music therapy and the higher your educational qualifications, the more job opportunities you'll have available to you. However, you don't have to earn a doctoral degree in music therapy to find a job, or necessarily even a master's degree.

If you become a certified music therapist, you could work with children who have communication issues or who have experienced trauma, for example.

Become a Certified Music Therapist

The Certification Board for Music Therapists (CBMT) offers a certification in music therapy, which you can take as soon as you've completed at least a bachelor's degree in music therapy as well as the required clinical training.

Medical Writer

If words are your creative outlet, then you might want to consider becoming a medical writer. There are two types of medical writers, according to the American Medical Writers Association (AMWA): those who produce scientific writing and those who write nonscientific texts.

Scientific medical authors write for a professional audience, such as doctors, scientists, or regulatory agencies such as the United States Food and Drug Administration (FDA).

Scientists, doctors, and medical professionals may be brilliant at what they do but they may not be particularly skilled at turning their work into understandable written language. Medical writers help them do that. They transform the technical work people have done into understandable written language. For scientific audiences, the level of complexity can be very high—much more complicated than the average reader can understand.

The other type of medical author writes for nonscientific audiences. They take that same complicated material from the scientists, doctors, and other healthcare professionals, and translate it into written work that the average person can understand. Sometimes that's for educational materials or press releases, and other times it's for advertisements or other purposes.

Career Insight:
Different Writing Styles for Different Audiences

Imagine that scientists have created a revolutionary new treatment for cancer. Medical professionals and the general public will both be interested in this drug, so both scientific medical writers and nonscientific medical writers will need to communicate the necessary information to that audience.

The scientific medical writer would handle writing the reports to be submitted to the FDA, so the drug can be approved for use. This report includes complex formulas, chemical breakdowns, and explanations of the parameters under which the drug was tested in the lab. These reports can be thousands of pages long because they must contain all the information about every aspect of the drug's usage and trials.

On the other hand, the nonscientific medical writer would handle writing a press release to make the public aware of the drug. The public wouldn't care about the chemical breakdowns and formulas or the testing parameters for the drug, so the writer wouldn't include any of that. Instead, the nonscientific medical writer would cover things like simple data on how the drug performed in trials (such as "99 percent of patients had no signs of cancer after four months of treatment with this drug") and possible side effects of the drug.

The role of medical writer is important—in this job, you would communicate important information, such as a scientific breakthrough.

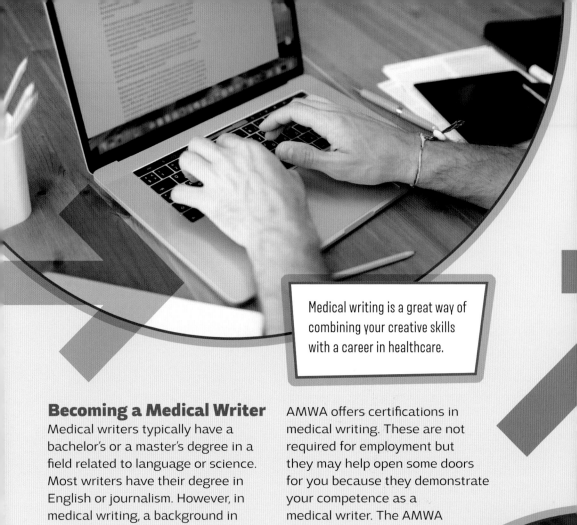

Medical writing is a great way of combining your creative skills with a career in healthcare.

Becoming a Medical Writer

Medical writers typically have a bachelor's or a master's degree in a field related to language or science. Most writers have their degree in English or journalism. However, in medical writing, a background in science is very helpful, so there are quite a few medical writers whose educational background is in science. They also happen to be skilled writers.

AMWA offers certifications in medical writing. These are not required for employment but they may help open some doors for you because they demonstrate your competence as a medical writer. The AMWA certifications are challenging, and passing them shows that you know what you're doing.

Being a freelance writer means that you can work from home and control your daily schedule to suit you.

Career Insight:
Freelance vs. In-House

Many careers in the healthcare field may require you to work in-house for a specific company or organization. This means that you go to work every day in the same office, for the same people, and receive your paycheck regularly. However, some careers in the healthcare field, such as medical writing, can be done as freelance work. That means you can work for a number of organizations at the same time in a self-employed role. When you consider a career in a field such as medical writing, where freelance work is possible, you'll have to make a decision as to whether you prefer that or in-house work.

Freelance employees can work for multiple companies or organizations. They often work at home, though sometimes they go into an office or facility. If they have several clients, this in-house work could be done for one or two days a week at each client. The work freelancers do may be the same as an in-house employee but the pay is a little different.

When you work in-house for one employer, taxes and contributions to Social Security and Medicare are taken out of your paycheck, and often your employer will also provide medical insurance for you (at a relatively reasonable cost, depending on the employer). If you work freelance, your clients don't take any taxes out of your paycheck—it's up to you to file and pay your taxes at the appropriate time. You'll also pay an additional 15.3 percent self-employment tax, which goes to cover contributions to Social Security and Medicare. Added to this, you'll have to find and pay for your own health insurance, which can be costly.

There are benefits to working freelance, though. You can choose which clients you want to work for. You often have much more flexibility in your schedule than you would as an in-house employee. However, if you don't work, you won't earn money. As a result, the pay rates are sometimes higher for freelance writers than for in-house staff.

A DAY IN THE LIFE OF
A Music Therapist

Music therapists are very often self-employed freelancers, so their days look vastly different—some work part-time, and others have a full day of clients. These pages provide an insight into what a day in the life of a music therapist might look like.

8:00 a.m. Your day usually starts with a morning jog or a session in the gym. While you love your job, you put a lot of yourself into it, and it's important that you take a little relaxation time just for you before the day begins.

It's amazing to see how music makes such a difference to the lives of your patients.

9:30 a.m. You arrive at the office at 9:30, ready to start the day. You teach classes and do one-on-one sessions at a facility that serves people with disabilities so you get to see a wide range of clients. You answer any email and voicemail messages before your first session.

10:00 a.m. Class begins! This one is for babies and toddlers. While some people wonder what children so young can get out of a music class, you're very aware of all the research supporting the fact that music helps make brain connections in the minds of young children. Plus, you love seeing the babies and toddlers!

11:00 a.m. Class over, you see your first one-on-one client: a young man with cerebral palsy. He loves music but struggles with motor control. You've found that plucking out tunes on a stringed instrument gives him some valuable exercise for his fine-motor skills.

12:00 p.m. Lesson done, you take a lunch break. You need some downtime before the afternoon appointments begin.

1:00 p.m. Your next one-on-one appointment arrives. This young girl had a stroke as a baby, which caused her to have difficulty speaking. She loves to sing and you've found that she can speak more clearly when you have her sing, so you have singing conversations back and forth, working on those speech motor skills.

2:00 p.m. Your next client is a woman with severe mental illness. Music calms her and allows her to express herself in ways that she is typically unable to do. Your sessions with her consist of her creating music with you gently guiding the direction. It's a go-with-your-gut kind of thing—you try to assess how she's feeling at any given time and guide the music to support her.

3:00 p.m. School's out for the day so now you can hold some more group classes. Your first one is a drum circle for elementary-aged children. They have a variety of different disabilities but they all enjoy participating in the drum circle, and it's a great way to build mind-body connections.

4:00 p.m. Your second class of the afternoon is for teens. It's a little like a jam session. Like the class before, the students in this class have a variety of disabilities. They all love making music and enjoy different instruments, so you have a jam band. Twice a year, you put on performances for their families.

5:00 p.m. You leave the office and head to a local nursing home. Once a week, you play music during the dinner hour for the residents. They love it, and you love seeing how some of the quieter ones really come alive and show such enjoyment when they hear the music.

Creator

Now that you've learned about some of the creator roles in healthcare, explore how you feel about each job a little more. Use the questions below to help you assess how strongly you feel each role might suit you.

Medical Illustrator

- Are you artistic but also love the structure and order of science? What other skills do you have that would make you a successful medical illustrator?
- Would you be prepared to work hard to get into one of the few medical illustrator courses? Are there things you could do to improve your chances of getting onto one of the courses?
- Some medical illustrators work for themselves as freelancers. What do you think are the advantages of working for yourself? And what might the disadvantages be?

Music Therapist

- What musical talents do you have?
- Why would you enjoy working with clients and being creative by using your musical talents to help them heal?
- Music therapists need to be good listeners and empathetic. What other personality traits and skills do you think they must have to be good at their jobs?
- Some music therapists travel from client to client. Is this something you would enjoy or would you prefer to work from your own office? Why do you say so?

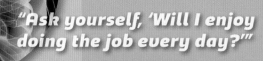

"Ask yourself, 'Will I enjoy doing the job every day?'"

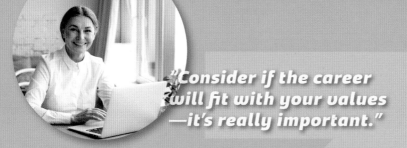

"Consider if the career will fit with your values —it's really important."

Medical Writer

- Being a writer can be a solitary job with little interaction with others. Would you find this challenging? If so, how would you deal with these challenges?
- Are you able to follow a brief and take instructions from clients? What particular skills do you have that would make you good at this?

"Think about the financial side of your chosen career—will it suit your lifestyle plans for the future?"

A DAY IN THE LIFE OF
A Music Therapist

- Review the Day in the Life feature. Did anything about the day surprise you? What was that?
- What do you think the challenges were, and how might you deal with them?
- What aspects of the role do you think you would enjoy?
- Look at the structure of the day and the working hours. Would you be happy with that structure? How might it affect your lifestyle?

Research More

If you like the idea of working as a creator in healthcare, but are not sure the jobs covered in this chapter suit you, here are some more creator roles you could explore.

Medical Photographer
Hospital Web Editor
Plastic Surgeon

CHAPTER FIVE

ORGANIZER ROLES IN HEALTHCARE

If you're the type of person who likes everything to be meticulously organized and to run efficiently, there are a number of jobs well suited to you in the healthcare field. In the hospital or a medical office, your organizational skills will be appreciated in whichever career you choose to use them. Let's take a look at options.

Healthcare Administrator

Healthcare administrators direct and coordinate healthcare services. In some cases, they manage a specific department of the hospital or medical office. In other cases, those who are very experienced may manage the entire hospital or healthcare facility.

Organization is an important skill in this position because healthcare administrators have a wide range of duties and they need to be on top of things. One of their most important duties is to be knowledgeable about new regulations, laws, and technologies. They must make sure

Hospitals and other healthcare facilities are hugely complex organizations. They require people with great organizational skills to make sure they run smoothly and efficiently.

Healthcare administrators often work with a large team of medical staff to ensure a hospital is meeting its targets.

that their department or facility is operating in compliance with all laws and regulations, and running as efficiently as possible. Failure to do this could result in heavy fines or even closure for the facility.

To make sure their facility is running smoothly, healthcare administrators are often in charge of recruiting and training new staff members. In some cases the human resources (HR) department may handle this but once new employees are on board, healthcare administrators supervise them and ensure that their work is up to the facility's standards of care. Healthcare administrators are often in charge of scheduling—they figure out which doctors are on shifts and when surgeries should be planned. Sometimes, they may also handle the facility's finances—even if a finance or billing department does a lot of the financial work, the healthcare administrator still has to oversee everything and sign off on it. Both of these duties require exceptional organizational skills.

When a face for the facility is needed at a public event, a board meeting, or another event, the healthcare administrator is usually the person who attends on behalf of the department or facility. Healthcare administrators who are in charge of a specific department at a larger facility act as the contact between staff members and the overall facility administration.

Healthcare administrators need at least a bachelor's degree to be eligible for the position, though in many cases a master's degree is required. Smaller facilities or departments may be willing to hire an administrator with a bachelor's degree and related experience but larger facilities generally have a large pool of applicants, many of whom have a master's degree. So if this is a field that interests you, you would be wise to plan on eventually completing a master's degree in any of the following options: healthcare administration, health management, public health administration, business administration, nursing, or a similar, related field.

Career Insight:
Financial Clerk

Being a financial clerk is an excellent job for people interested in working in healthcare and who have strong organizational skills and an aptitude for working with figures. This position exists in many fields, with healthcare being just one of them. In healthcare settings, financial clerks need to be especially organized and methodical because medical billing can be very complex: Patients have different insurance plans and medical facilities have to deal with insurance billings, patient copays, and more. Financial clerks are responsible for maintaining financial records, determining billing and charges for patients, and explaining the sometimes complicated billing that results when insurance companies are involved.

They need to be very thorough in case there is a discrepancy between the insurance company and the healthcare facility.

Some financial clerks don't work in the patient side of things. Instead, they work in payroll. In that case, they're responsible for recording employees' hours worked and making sure employees get paid for them.

One great aspect of becoming a financial clerk is that it doesn't require any schooling beyond high school—training is usually done on the job. Different healthcare facilities use different computerized billing and financial systems, so they are generally willing to train their financial clerks in whatever system they use.

Healthcare facilities are often run on huge budgets that require great planning.

Recording medical data about patients on their medical records requires an eye for detail and meticulous administration skills.

Health Information Technician

If you're looking for a career in the healthcare field in which you can put your organizational skills to good use without necessarily having to earn a bachelor's or a master's degree, you might want to consider becoming a health information technician.

Health information technicians are the people who keep patient information organized. For example, they review patient records for completeness and accuracy and then make sure that patient information is entered and tracked in databases and registries. They use specific software to code patient information, so that the medical facility is reimbursed by the insurance company for patient care costs. They also code what the patients are seen for, which helps for tracking purposes. For example, every year during flu season, medical facilities track the number of flu cases they see. This helps them document when the flu season has peaked. Health information technicians also sometimes track patient outcomes for research purposes. Until a cure is found for diseases such as cancer, an important part of the healthcare field is tracking treatment of patients and their survival outcome. That is how they learn which treatments are most effective and which aren't. So, for simple patient issues such as a broken bone, a lot of follow-up is not required from a research standpoint but for conditions such as cancer, medical facilities like to keep meticulous records on how patients respond after their treatment.

Ensuring Patient Confidentiality

Health information technicians are also in charge of ensuring patient confidentiality. The Health Insurance Portability and Accountability Act (HIPAA) was signed into law in 1996. It places strict regulations on medical facilities to ensure that patient records are kept private and confidential. Any violation of HIPAA can open the facility to a possible lawsuit, which could cost millions of dollars. So while keeping patient records confidential sounds like a small part of a health information technician's job, it's an extremely important part and needs to be done with the utmost care.

Depending on the healthcare facility, you might be able to get a position as a health information technician with just a high school diploma and previous experience in the field. In many cases, it would be beneficial to have taken at least some postsecondary coursework in health information technology (IT). There are also associate degree programs in this field, which can help improve how you are perceived by potential employers. You'll also want to earn a certification in the field. There are several possible certifications and most involve passing an exam. If you've taken the postsecondary coursework, it should prepare you for the certification.

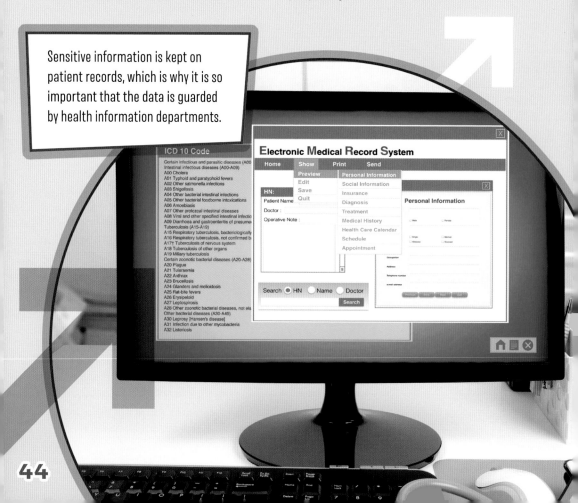

Sensitive information is kept on patient records, which is why it is so important that the data is guarded by health information departments.

Health and safety technicians ensure that healthcare workers are provided with suitably protective equipment.

Career Insight:
Health and Safety

If you're a detail-oriented person, being an occupational health and safety technician might be perfect for you. In the general workplace, these technicians measure hazards and conduct tests to make sure workers and the public are safe and taking the correct precautions to limit injury and illness in the workplace. For example, on a construction site, the technician would need to ensure that all workers are using protective eyewear, safety shoes, and hard hats. In the healthcare field, patient and healthcare safety is also incredibly important, so being a health and safety technician is a crucially important role.

Occupational health and safety technicians help make sure everyone is safe in the healthcare environment. For example, during the Covid-19 pandemic, the occupational health and safety technicians had to be certain that all healthcare frontline workers were aware of the risks involved and that they wore correct personal protective equipment (PPE) to limit their risk of contracting the highly infectious virus.

In addition to being organized, you'll need to be a good problem solver and generally concerned for others and their safety and wellbeing. In general, occupational health and safety technicians need to have only a high school diploma and their training for the position can be done on the job. However, there are associate's degrees in occupational health and safety and certificate programs available from some community colleges. As with any role, further studying often opens up more job possibilities.

A DAY IN THE LIFE OF
A Hospital Administrator

Hospital administrators have a lot of duties in any given day—it's busy and there's a lot of problem solving involved. Let's take a look at how a typical day might look for a hospital administrator.

8:00 a.m. Hospitals are difficult to run, and you have a lot to accomplish in a day. You start by answering voicemails and emails from the night before. There are always a lot of emails—sometimes, you're directly involved but in other cases, the sender is copying you in for reference. Either way, you need to remember this information so that you are always on top of things.

9:00 a.m. You attend a budget meeting with the heads of each department. You've been working on the annual budget for several days, and the next step is to get financial updates from each department. It shouldn't be a difficult task as your heads of department are always organized and efficient.

10:00 a.m. The meeting ended right on time, so you go back to your office to start inputting the numbers each department head gave you. The trauma department wasn't at the meeting, so you have everyone else's numbers but you need to get hers. You search the hospital for her, because she hasn't responded to your emails. The trauma department is always busy, so it's easier to handle things yourself.

11:30 a.m. The trauma head was easy to track down, and she promises to send you her numbers later in the day. You decide to grab something to eat before continuing your day.

12:00 p.m. The president of the hospital board calls. There's an emergency board meeting this evening that you'll have to attend. A patient is filing a malpractice lawsuit and the board needs to strategize for how to handle it. You set to work researching every detail of the patient's history with the hospital and put in calls to the physicians who worked with the patient. You'll need to get their story about what happened before the board meeting.

1:00 p.m. You drop by the staff meeting for the nurses. Usually, you leave these things to the nurse managers but there's been a policy change in how nursing shifts are assigned at the hospital, and that news should come from you so you can field any questions about it.

2:00 p.m. The nursing meeting is done, and it appears the head of trauma has sent you her financial reports, so you enter that into the system and look at the overall numbers for the hospital budget. They don't look quite as good as you'd hoped, so cost-cutting is going to have to happen somewhere. After poring over the numbers for a while, you have some ideas about where costs could be cut but you'll need to talk to the department heads in question

Every day is busy in your role because your job involves working with many different departments and their staff.

and see whether they can indeed make do with a slightly smaller budget. They won't be thrilled about it but hopefully they can manage. You ask your assistant to schedule meetings with those department heads over the next couple of days.

3:00 p.m. You head to the OR observation area to watch an innovative surgery taking place. You don't often spend time watching surgeries but this particular operation has never been done before and everyone is excited to see it in action. If your hospital becomes known for innovation, it can only mean good things for everyone.

3:30 p.m. You drag yourself away, even though the surgery was really exciting to watch, because you still need to talk to the physicians

who worked with the patient who is suing the hospital. Now that it's late in the afternoon, they're likely to have a few minutes to talk.

5:00 p.m. With all your facts in order and the information at hand, you head to the board meeting. During the meeting, you present your facts to the board. The board and the hospital's attorneys are fairly certain that the patient has a valid case, so the hospital has decided to make a settlement offer rather than go through court. Now all that remains is to see whether the patient accepts the generous offer of settlement the hospital is prepared to make. You wish this hadn't happened, but doctors are human and mistakes happen.

6:30 p.m. You finally head home, tired but pleased with the work you completed.

Organizer

Now that you've learned about some of the organizer roles in healthcare, explore more about how you feel about each job. Use the questions below to help you assess how strongly you feel each role might suit you.

Healthcare Administrator

- What is it that you find interesting about the role of a healthcare administrator?
- Would you be happy to manage a large team of people and make sure they are completing their jobs well and on time? How would you deal with those staff members who are not?
- What skills do you have to help you manage large budgets?

Health Information Technician

- This job requires organizational skills as well as discretion. What other skills and traits would you need to do the job?
- You would need to work with medical insurance companies. Would you find this challenging? Why do you say so?
- What do you think the other challenges of this role are, and do you have particular skills that might help you deal with them?

"Always keep an eye on the future and how your career might change. For example, will technological advancements change some aspects of your job?"

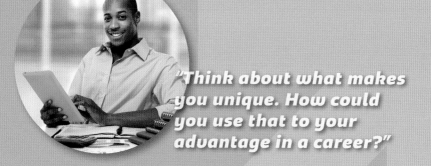

"Think about what makes you unique. How could you use that to your advantage in a career?"

A DAY IN THE LIFE OF
A Hospital Administrator

- Review the Day in the Life feature. Did anything about the day surprise you? What was that?
- What do you think the challenges were, and how might you deal with them?
- What aspects of the role do you think you would enjoy?
- Look at the structure of the day and the working hours. Would you be happy with that structure? How might it affect your lifestyle?

"Never rush into career decisions. Always take your time, and work through all your options."

Research More

If you like the idea of working as an organizer in healthcare, but are not sure the jobs covered in this chapter suit you, here are some more organizer roles you could explore.

Vaccination Manager
Operations Manager
Clinical Trial Assistant

CHAPTER SIX

THINKER ROLES IN HEALTHCARE

If the results of the flowchart earlier in this book identified your career type as thinker, you're probably someone who likes to know all the information, analyze the details, and draw careful conclusions about things. These are excellent skills to have in the healthcare field, and there are a number of career paths that would be very well suited to you.

Pathologist

Pathologists are medical doctors who specialize in the study of disease. They look at blood and tissue samples and help doctors diagnose patients' illnesses and conditions. For example, an oncologist (a doctor who treats patients with cancer) might suspect that their patient has cancer but the pathologist is the one who can confirm it. The pathologist studies tissue samples taken during a biopsy. A biopsy is an examination of a tissue sample removed from a body to determine whether it is diseased or healthy tissue. It determines if the patient has cancer and, if so, exactly

The work of a pathologist is ideally suited to people with thinker personalities, who enjoy working through problems and carrying out detective work to solve them.

Becoming a pathologist requires intensive study but that often suits thinkers, who enjoy research and analysis. The knowledge they acquire through their rigorous training helps prepare them for a job that involves examining complicated cases.

what type of cancer the patient has. In this way, pathologists are like detectives in the healthcare field. They have to look at evidence in the form of tissue, blood, or urine samples, and determine exactly what is going on in the patient's body.

The field of pathology is a job for thinkers because pathologists need to be able to think outside of the box. Sometimes, the samples they see have very obvious markers for a particular disease or condition but other times, a patient may have a rare disease or disorder that isn't often seen, and the pathologist has to dig deep into their knowledge to figure out what the problem is.

At times, pathologists also complete autopsies. An autopsy is performed when the cause of a patient's death is uncertain or suspicious in some way. An autopsy is an examination of a dead body to find out the cause

of death. Patients who are expected to die, whether from disease or old age, for example, don't generally have autopsies but if a younger person with no known serious health conditions dies, an autopsy may be performed. In this case, the pathologist again has to be a detective. They have to look at every inch of the body to see if they can determine what caused the person's death.

To become a pathologist, you'll need to study to be a doctor by earning a bachelor's degree and completing four years of medical school. Once you've passed the certifications, you will also need to complete a residency, which is normally four years for pathologists. Some pathologists who want to specialize in a certain part of the field will also complete a fellowship, which generally lasts one to two years. You will need to be certified through the American Board of Pathology (ABP).

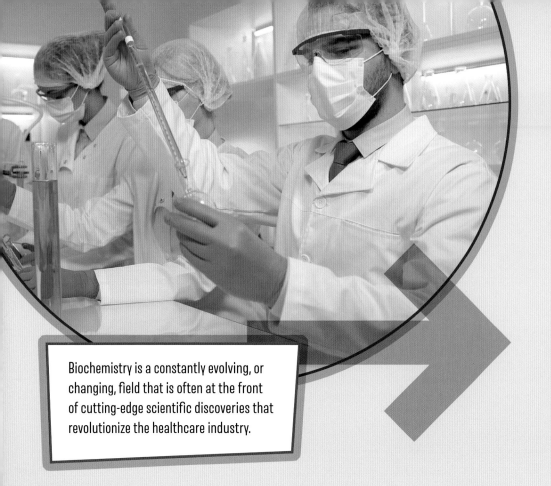

Biochemistry is a constantly evolving, or changing, field that is often at the front of cutting-edge scientific discoveries that revolutionize the healthcare industry.

Biochemist

If you're a thinker, research might be very appealing to you. Biochemists are one type of researcher in the healthcare field. They work in labs and study living things and biological processes. For example, they may research the effects of nutrients or drugs on cells, tissues, and biological processes. In recent years, much research has been done on genetics, deoxyribonucleic acid (DNA), and disease. For example, biochemists working in cancer research work on projects such as targeted drug therapies that can isolate and attack cancer cells, rather than destroying a person's entire immune system, which is how cancer used to be treated. They also work on new ventures such as gene splicing to try to help people's bodies better fight diseases.

Biochemistry is an exciting and very important field that requires a lot of education. Most biochemists have a bachelor's degree in biochemistry or a related field, and they then go on to earn their PhD in biochemistry or a specialized or related field. Biochemists also need to be prepared to publish their findings in research journals and to share their work in the lab with other professionals.

Biological Technician

If you're interested in working in a research lab but you don't necessarily want to earn a PhD, you could become a biological technician. In this role, you would work in labs and assist biochemists and other researchers with their work. Biological technicians do everything from cleaning and setting up lab equipment to preparing the biological samples the researchers will be working with to actually carrying out tests and experiments. They also assist with data collection because researchers must have meticulous data records to be able to analyze their work and assess the outcomes from it.

Biological technicians generally need to have a bachelor's degree in biology or a related field. Occasionally, there are positions available to those without a degree if they have lab experience but in most cases, a degree is required.

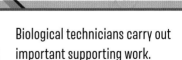

Biological technicians carry out important supporting work.

Laboratory work lends itself to a huge number of different industries, so becoming qualified in this area could open up a wide number of career options for you.

Career Insight:
Helping the Environment

If research on human diseases and processes is not something you would like to do, but you're still interested in research in the healthcare field, it is worth noting that biochemists also work in other interesting areas. For example, some biochemists carry out research on alternative energy sources or on ways to lessen pollution. If the environment is your passion, there are ways to use a biochemistry background to benefit the natural world.

Laboratory Technologist

If you're interested in a career that requires careful study but doesn't require a medical degree or other advanced education, you might want to consider becoming a medical laboratory technologist. In this role, you would perform complex tests and procedures to help other healthcare professionals. This may include looking at blood, urine, and tissue samples, and then analyzing any abnormalities in them.

Once a lab technologist has analyzed samples, they then log their findings in the patient's medical record. They may need to discuss their findings with the patient's physician, if there's anything out of the ordinary or unexpected. In some healthcare facilities, technologists perform many different types of analysis but in other facilities, the technologists may specialize in certain types of analysis. For example, in blood banks, technologists analyze blood samples for transfusion. Their work will include determining the blood type, the number of cells in a sample, and the blood's compatibility with other blood types. They may also look for markers for disease, such as HIV or malaria, to make sure the blood is safe to give to patients that require a blood transfusion.

Medical laboratory technologists usually need to have a bachelor's degree in medical technology, life science, or a related field. In addition, depending on what state you work in, you might need to earn a certification. Usually, to be able to take the certification exam, you must have taken the suggested coursework.

If earning a bachelor's degree isn't in your current plan but this career sounds interesting, you might want to become a medical laboratory technician instead. That job typically only requires an associate's degree or a certificate. The level of work is not as complicated as that of a technologist, for example, a technician may prepare the samples for the technologist or may do basic tests, such as looking for urinary tract infections in a urine sample. However, to become a laboratory technician, you may still need to be certified, depending on the state you work in.

Becoming a laboratory technician could provide you with a relatively quick route into healthcare.

A DAY IN THE LIFE OF
A Pathologist

In any healthcare profession, each day is unique. Although pathologists see a lot of different cases in any given week, these pages will give you an idea of how their typical day looks.

8:00 a.m. You arrive in your office for the day and respond to any emails or voicemails that have come in since yesterday. There are always at least a few questions to answer.

8:30 a.m. The day's work begins with reviewing samples that have been prepared for you. There are several polyps, or growths, removed during routine colonoscopies, as well as cervical smears to check for female cancers, and a biopsy to check for breast cancer. Not everything you screen is for cancer, but colon, reproductive, and breast cancers are fairly common, so a lot of your screens are looking for those types of cancer.

10:00 a.m. It's time for the Multidisciplinary Team (MDT) meeting. This is when you meet with specialists from other disciplines to form a treatment plan for patients whose screens have come back with an illness that requires treatment. Surgeons, radiologists, oncologists, and pathologists all present their views on each case and work together to find the best treatment plan for each patient. As a pathologist, your job is to discuss any

Although your job can be demanding and intense, it is rewarding and constantly stimulating, which suits your enquiring mind.

A lot of your work is carried out alone in isolation, so attending meetings such as the MDTs provides you with a chance to work with others and exchange ideas.

specific markers you saw in the tissue and/or blood samples that would indicate one particular treatment plan would be better than another.

12:00 p.m. The MDT meeting is sobering—after all, you're discussing patients who have serious illnesses and could die from them if not treated correctly. And, even with the correct treatment, they could still have a terminal illness.

12:45 p.m. You grab some lunch and head back to your office. There are more samples waiting to be analyzed. You work in a hospital, so every day is a constant flow of samples that need to be analyzed, and many doctors want to be sure it's done right immediately. There are only so many you can do right now, but you try to keep on top of them and keep everyone happy.

3:00 p.m. It's time for the afternoon meeting with the other pathologists in the lab. The lab has one multiheaded microscope that allows several people to look at a sample at the same time, so you have a short daily meeting where you can all look at more difficult slides and brainstorm what might be going on in them. Today, there's one with what appears to be a sample showing a very rare parasitic infection.

While that's not good news for the patient, it is certainly interesting to see from a pathology standpoint.

3:30 p.m. You end your day looking at the larger samples, such as sections of intestines removed from patients with diseased colons. You have to look at several smaller samples of these large pieces, so you often spend the last part of your day preparing the smaller samples for the next morning. You examine the large pieces as a whole, record your observations, and then carefully trim small pieces out and mount them on slides. You'll examine those slides under the microscope tomorrow morning and wrap up your report on the samples.

5:00 p.m. You head home for the day. Of course, there are more samples to be examined, but it's a hospital, so there is a staff member on duty overnight to look at urgent samples. You are free to go home and enjoy your evening.

Thinker

Now that you've learned about some of the thinker roles in healthcare, explore more about how you feel about each job. Use the questions below to help you assess how strongly you feel each role might suit you.

Pathologist

- What would you find challenging about this job? What can you do to overcome these challenges?
- Working as a pathologist can often be solitary. Is this something you would enjoy? Why do you say so?
- Pathologists have to work under pressure to deliver important results. Are you good at this? If not, how can you improve?

Biochemist

- Would you be prepared to spend a long time studying to be a biochemist?
- What aspects of the job do you think you would enjoy? Why?
- Are there parts of this role that you would find challenging? Would you enjoy those challenges?
- To be a biochemist, you need to be methodical, organized, and able to work well under pressure. What other skills do you have that will help you do this job?

"Close your eyes and picture yourself doing your ideal job in the future. What type of workplace setting are you in and what are you doing? Keep that vision in mind as you research careers."

"Write down your top five strengths and weaknesses on a piece of paper. Keep it to hand and use it to help you work through career options."

Biological Technician

- Would you enjoy working as a member of a medical team and helping others to do their jobs?
- Keeping medical records up to date is an important part of the job. What skills would you need to do this?

Laboratory Technologist

- In this job, you would need to prepare and analyze samples to help other medical professionals. Would that suit you? Why?
- Could you work as a member of a team?

"Once you know what career you'd like to follow, make a flowchart that shows all the steps you need to take to get to that career —then follow it!"

Research More

If you like the idea of working as a thinker in healthcare, but are not sure the jobs covered in this chapter suit you, here are some more thinker roles you could explore.

Psychologist
Food Scientist and Technologist
Microbiologist

WHAT NEXT?—YOUR CAREER CHECKLIST

If you have come to the end of this book and are ready to start making a career in healthcare a reality, follow the checklist on these pages to kick-start your future.

Start at School

All roles in healthcare will require strong science skills, so focus on your science classes at school. Many healthcare roles also require strong math and communication skills, so focus on your English and math classes too.

If you are interested in builder roles, ask if your school offers some vocational courses as options, such as computer-aided design and drafting (CADD) or computer science courses that include robotics, and make sure you sign up for them. You will develop useful skills that you can use in a builder role, for example, if you become a product builder.

Creator roles in healthcare will allow you to mix your creative talents with your interest in healthcare. Choose subjects at school that will help you develop this career area. For example, studying visual arts at school will help you carve out a career in medical illustration, and if you are interested in moving into music therapy, studying music will of course be essential.

If you are interested in organizer roles, ask if your school offers IT courses as options. In those courses, you'll become familiar with different aspects of the type of skills you'll likely need in an organizer role, such as learning to use word-processing software and spreadsheets.

Talk to a Guidance Counselor

If your guidance counselor offers career advice, take it! Guidance counselors will be able to help you explore a lot of different options and talk more about whether a role in healthcare could suit you. They will also be able to advise you on further education courses you could pursue after school or in-job training that could suit you.

Get Connected

Your parents and parents' friends may have great contacts in the healthcare world. They may be able to put you in touch with an employer, so that you can talk to them directly about roles in healthcare that interest you. For example, a parent or friend could connect you with a residential healthcare provider, so that you can talk to the people who work there about the roles they carry out.

Walk in Their Shoes

Some employers are happy to have students meet with them in person for informational interviews, through which you can find out what people in healthcare roles do. You may even be able to shadow someone who works in healthcare. Talking to people who actually work in the job is a great way to discover if you would like to do their role in the future.

Get Experience

The best way to find out if a career is really going to suit you is to try it out! However, because roles in healthcare naturally require a significant amount of training before a person can start working in the field, you will not be able to get real work experience until you start your training in your chosen area. At that point, you may be able to get an internship position—an unpaid temporary role in which people gain work experience. Internships provide real-world experience, which is invaluable to students training in healthcare.

Do Your Research

You can never do enough research when it comes to planning a future career, so explore as many resources as you can to find out more. Start by taking a look at the resources on page 63 of this book to learn more. For example, the U.S. Bureau of Labor Statistics (BLS) offers some great resources that can help you learn more about possible roles in healthcare. Check out in particular their Occupational Outlook Handbook section.

As you research, remember there is never a right or wrong in making choices, and you can always change your mind. Keep flexible, be positive about your future, and have fun choosing your perfect STEM career.

analysis detailed examination of something, usually for the purpose of drawing conclusions

associate's degree a two-year degree awarded by a community college

cholecystectomy the surgical removal of the bladder

colonoscopy a nonsurgical procedure that allows a physician to examine a patient's large intestine

copay a patient's portion of their medical bills, as opposed to the amount their insurance pays

dentures artificial teeth on a removable plate that fits inside the mouth

deoxyribonucleic acid (DNA) the carrier of each living organism's genetic code

diabetes a disease in which the body is unable to produce or respond to insulin

GED a set of exams that allows students who pass them to receive a credential equivalent to a high school diploma

genetics the study of inherited characteristics

glucose monitors monitors that show the levels of glucose in a person's body

malpractice insurance insurance that protects an individual who is sued for negligent or improper care

medicare a federal program providing health insurance to people over age 65 or who have certain disabilities

motor skills a learned ability to cause a predetermined movement. Walking, jumping, and writing are all examples of motor skills

oncologist a doctor who specializes in the treatment of cancer

orthotics the medical field that deals with artificial devices, such as splints and braces

PhD a doctoral degree in a field other than medicine

podiatry the treatment of the feet and their ailments

postsecondary refers to education beyond high school

rehabilitation related to the medical treatment of patients in order to regain their health or mobility after injury or illness

residency a period in which future physicians receive specialized medical training in a hospital

samples small sections of tissue

Social Security a federal program that provides benefits to qualifying people who are retired, unemployed, or disabled

terminal illness an illness that will result in death

transfusion the transfer of donated blood into the circulatory system of another person

trauma a deeply upsetting experience

vocational school a school that is designed to teach the skills necessary for certain occupations

Books

Brezina, Corona. *Jump-Starting a Career in Ultrasound and Sonography* (Health Care Careers in 2 Years). Rosen Young Adult, 2019.

Harmon, Daniel. *Jump-Starting a Career in Optometry and Ophthalmology* (Health Care Careers in 2 Years). Rosen Young Adult, 2019.

Oxlade, Chris. *Dream Jobs in Health* (Cutting-Edge Careers in STEM). Crabtree Publishing Company, 2017.

Porterfield, Jason. *Jump-Starting a Career in Radiology* (Health Care Careers in 2 Years). Rosen Young Adult, 2019.

Websites

Take a look at the BLS site for more careers guidance:
www.bls.gov/k12/students/careers/how-can-bls-help-me-explore-careers.htm

Check out the BLS Occupational Outlook Handbook to find out more about different jobs and the qualifications you need for them:
www.bls.gov/ooh

This site allows you to assess your strengths, explore different industries, and plan for a career that fits your passion. Take a look at:
www.cacareerzone.org

Sponsored by the United States Department of Labor, this website is a one-stop shop for everything you want to know about careers. There are videos and resources about many different career options.
www.careeronestop.org

This website connects teens with experiential learning opportunities, including summer programs, community service opportunities, and other programs:
www.teenlife.com

Publisher's note to educators and parents:
All the websites featured above have been carefully reviewed to ensure that they are suitable for students. However, many websites change often, and we cannot guarantee that a site's future contents will continue to meet our high standards of educational value. Please be advised that students should be closely monitored whenever they access the Internet.

INDEX

About the Author

Cathleen Small has written many books for young people on a wide variety of topics. In writing this book she has learned the value of personality testing, research, and considering many options when exploring a future career.